BRITISH G
DRESS

OCCUPATIONAL CLOTHING 1750–1950

Jayne Shrimpton

SHIRE PUBLICATIONS

Published in Great Britain in 2012 by Shire Publications Ltd, Midland House, West Way, Botley, Oxford OX2 0PH, United Kingdom.

44-02 23rd Street, Suite 219, Long Island City, NY 11101, USA.

E-mail: shire@shirebooks.co.uk   www.shirebooks.co.uk

© 2012 Jayne Shrimpton.

All rights reserved. Apart from any fair dealing for the purpose of private study, research, criticism or review, as permitted under the Copyright, Designs and Patents Act, 1988, no part of this publication may be reproduced, stored in a retrieval system, or transmitted in any form or by any means, electronic, electrical, chemical, mechanical, optical, photocopying, recording or otherwise, without the prior written permission of the copyright owner. Enquiries should be addressed to the Publishers.

Every attempt has been made by the Publishers to secure the appropriate permissions for materials reproduced in this book. If there has been any oversight we will be happy to rectify the situation and a written submission should be made to the Publishers.

A CIP catalogue record for this book is available from the British Library.

Shire Library no. 702.   ISBN-13: 978 0 74781 197 8

Jayne Shrimpton has asserted her right under the Copyright, Designs and Patents Act, 1988, to be identified as the author of this book.

Designed by Tony Truscott Designs, Sussex, UK and typeset in Perpetua and Gill Sans.

Printed in China through Worldprint Ltd.

12 13 14 15 16   10 9 8 7 6 5 4 3 2 1

COVER IMAGE

Work by Ford Maddox Brown, 1862–5, from Manchester City Art Galleries, depicts Victorian navvies labouring in shirt sleeves, their rolled-up trousers teamed with high-laced hobnail boots. One wears a striped stocking (or brewers') cap.

TITLE PAGE IMAGE

Fishermen on a Hull trawler shortly before the First World War wear a variety of clothing, including ganseys, 'slop' shirts and jackets, heavy-duty canvas trousers, and leather boots.

CONTENTS PAGE IMAGE

Until females were prohibited from working down mines, many older girls pulled coal trucks wearing only flimsy half-shifts, as seen in this illustration from the 1842 Children's Employment Commission's report.

ACKNOWLEDGEMENTS

I am grateful for the help and support of many individuals and organisations in the production of this book, especially those who have generously contributed images from their personal or professional picture collections. In particular I should like to thank:

Fiona Adams, 47 (top); Ashley Birch Collection/British Tramway Company Buttons and Badges, pages 37, 38 (left and right); Agnes Burton, page 30 (right); Maddy Cook, page 30 (left); Richard Coomber, page 11 (bottom); Ron Cosens/Victorian Image Collection, pages 20, 27 (top), 29, 43 (right), 50 (bottom), 52 (bottom); Patrick Davison, page 41; Jacqueline Depelle, page 26 (top); Jon Easter, page 61 (bottom); James Feely, page 39 (all); Dr. Melanie Fraser, page 44 (top left); The Geffrye Museum/The Bridgeman Art Library, page 22; Barrie Green/Barrie's Fire Helmets, page 42 (left); Mike Greenop, page 26 (bottom); Dr Gerald Hargreaves, page 53; Manchester City Art Galleries/The Bridgeman Art Library, page 48; Manx Museum, Isle of Man, pages 11 (top), 17; Mary Evans Picture Library, pages 16 (bottom), 21, 32, 43 (left); Jon Mills, pages 12–13 (all), 36 (all), 42 (right), 44 (top right, bottom), 46, 54 (top right, bottom); James Morley/Whatsthatpicture, title page, pages 10, 58 (top right); The Museum of English Rural Life, Reading, page 8; The National Gallery of Wales/The Bridgeman Art Library, page 18; National Museums, Liverpool/The Bridgeman Art Library, page 9 (top); The National Trust/The Bridgeman Art Library, page 25; Norland College, page 31 (bottom); Sue Peyman-Stroud, pages 47 (bottom), 58 (left); Peter Rigarlsford/PSV Badges, page 35 (top, right); Richard Rosa, page 38 (middle); The Sutcliffe Gallery, page 14; Topfoto, front cover image; Katharine Williams, pages 27 (bottom), 54 (top left), 60 (bottom).

All W. H. Pyne costume plates were supplied by Shire; all other photographs are from the author's collection.

Shire Publications is supporting the Woodland Trust, the UK's leading woodland conservation charity, by funding the dedication of trees.

CONTENTS

INTRODUCTION

IN PAST ERAS, when the average person's wardrobe was less varied than today, work clothing was essentially a practical version of everyday dress. Historically, working garments broadly followed the lines of fashion but were made from coarse, sturdy materials that were cheaper than fine fabrics and better suited to regular, heavy use. Labouring men and women modified their dress by shedding outer layers for strenuous tasks, wearing shorter garments than fashion dictated, and avoiding exaggerated features that would impede movement, such as cumbersome dress hoops. Aprons, worn by many workers to protect their clothes, were also useful for carrying the day's food, tools of trade, or goods to market. Regional variations in dress existed throughout Britain, and some items were associated with specific occupations, for example the blacksmith's leather apron.

This book covers the period from the mid-eighteenth century to the mid-twentieth, during which time there was a shift away from traditional, mainly rural occupations to industrialisation and the growth of urban working environments. Significant advances in workwear during these years included the evolution of functional garments such as the farmworker's smock and early forms of trousers, the development of new durable and waterproof materials, and the introduction of basic safety gear for hazardous jobs. Some women devised unique working outfits that boldly defied convention and pre-empted fashion, while public services and the transport system increasingly used various formal uniforms for civilian jobs.

The sources used for this book embrace contemporary literary accounts, published books, specialist websites, surviving costume, and, above all, visual images ranging from paintings, through prints and engravings, to photographs. Military uniforms are not included, nor has it been possible to consider the clothing of all categories of workers, but many occupations are covered in these pages. The dress of our ordinary, hard-working ancestors demonstrates how they adapted to the physical demands of daily toil and the changing workplace, and how they appeared to their contemporaries, adding a fascinating dimension to our understanding of everyday life in the past.

Opposite:
This elderly farm labourer from Southwick, West Sussex, photographed c. 1900, wears a casual slop jacket with a shabby corduroy waistcoat and trousers and leather gaiters.

AGRICULTURE

GEORGIAN ENGLAND was more prosperous than Scotland, Wales, Ireland and much of continental Europe, and foreign visitors often observed how well-dressed English agricultural workers were, by comparison. In 1748 the Scandinavian horticulturalist Pehr Kalm was surprised to see Hertfordshire labourers wearing periwigs, and in 1782 a German pastor, Karl Philipp Moritz, remarked on Berkshire farmers' good, metropolitan-style garments and the lack of barefoot peasants in the fields. Such accounts may be simplistic, but historians agree that English country dress was fairly sophisticated by the mid- to late eighteenth century.

MEN

In the eighteenth and early nineteenth centuries male farmworkers wore knee breeches fashioned from sturdy cloth or, commonly, buckskin. Breeches were typically left undone at the knee for easier movement, while laced or strapped-on leather gaiters often protected the lower legs. Footwear ranged from stout shoes reinforced by soles studded with iron nails, through short boots called 'highlows' or 'startups', to leather-topped wooden clogs. Labourers might discard their coats and work in shirt sleeves, especially in summer, but throughout much of England and parts of Wales practical, protective 'smock frocks' or shorter smock-like garments were commonly worn over the clothes.

During the 1810s trousers became part of fashionable dress and, although some conservative or poorer workers still wore knee breeches for many years, gradually these were replaced by trousers. Like breeches, trousers could be made of buckskin, although fustian, moleskin and corduroy were becoming widely used as hard-wearing materials for men's work clothes. Gaiters were less commonly worn with trousers, but labourers often hitched up their trousers below the knee with a buckled strap, length of string, bootlace or straw, to free the knees, raise the hems out of the mud, and, allegedly, prevent field mice running up the leg. These devices were variously called 'yorks', 'bowy-yanks', 'lijahs', 'pitseas' and 'whirlers' in different areas, terms deriving from local dialect words for leggings or gaiters.

Opposite:
A woman churning butter, illustrated in W. H. Pyne's *Costume of Great Britain* (1805), wears typical late-Georgian female workwear: a bedgown, coloured petticoat, patterned neckerchief, apron and mob cap.

SMOCKS

The smock, the garment that typifies the English countryside more than any other, was a significant dress item between the eighteenth and early twentieth centuries. Some farm carters had adopted loose, smock-like linen or canvas coats in the seventeenth century, and these probably inspired the long-sleeved 'smock frock' or smock recorded by the mid-eighteenth century. Designed to protect the wearer from the elements and prevent clothes underneath from becoming dirty, the affordable, comfortable smock was a loose garment that usually extended to the knee or calf, and came in three main styles: a round, reversible smock put on over the head; a shirt-type version with a partial front opening at the chest; and an open, coat-like full-buttoning smock. Using several yards of fabric and generally made of linen, cotton or drabbet, most smocks were cream, beige, stone or buff in colour, while brown, green and blue smocks seem to have been regional variants.

Smocks were chiefly (though not exclusively) male garments, and their use varied with the job, location and occasion: worn in the Midlands, the South of England and in some parts of Wales, they were particularly favoured by shepherds, drovers, carters and waggoners, who worked outdoors in all weather, but they were also worn by

A farmworker's smock from Hungerford, Berkshire, c. 1885, from the collection of the Museum of English Rural Life, Reading.

other land workers, from gardeners to ferreters. Smocks were not, however, suitable for certain tasks or when working with farm machinery, their loose folds being potentially dangerous. Smocks first developed their distinctive honeycomb embroidery at the end of the eighteenth century, complex decorative stitching reaching its height around the mid-nineteenth century. The most elaborate embroidered examples surviving in museum collections were perhaps worn for weddings and 'Sunday best', rather than for work, but the practical everyday smock was a familiar sight in the countryside for much of our period. From the mid-nineteenth century onwards, smocks gradually declined in favour of more modern workwear, but the traditional smock lingered on in some areas and was still worn as late as the 1920s and 1930s, for example by shepherds in parts of Norfolk, Suffolk and Sussex.

With the gradual decline of the smock and the growing preference for trousers, the Victorian farmworker's dress evolved into a practical version of the urban male suit. Typically, a jacket or jerkin and waistcoat were worn over a collarless shirt, the jacket removed for strenuous tasks, and a neckerchief often tied around the neck. Jackets and waistcoats were made from flannel, or, like trousers, from corduroy or moleskin. For summer, an unbleached drill or lightweight canvas jacket was popular by the late nineteenth century, a casual garment generally called a 'slop', 'sloppy', or in the North a 'kitle'. In wet weather leather boots were sometimes given a waterproof dressing of

Scenes such as George Stubbs's *Haymakers*, 1794, from the Lady Lever Art Gallery, National Museums Liverpool, may be idealised, but support eighteenth-century observations that some farmworkers appeared well-dressed.

candle grease, while a hay lining inside provided extra warmth. Various hats of felt, animal hair or straw were often broad-brimmed, while in wintry conditions a fleecy overcoat might be worn by shepherds, drovers and others working outdoors. The nature of certain tasks inspired some rural craftsmen to devise special protective accessories: for example, hedgers working with thorny branches wore thick leather hedging mittens, and often coarse sacking smocks or aprons, while thatchers usually wore protective leather knee pads strapped around the trousers.

Victorian-style working garments and materials remained common until the First World War, after which more modern garments and materials gradually became available. Wellington boots with waterproof linings were in use by the 1920s and, although slow to be adopted nationwide, eventually replaced leather boots and gaiters. Jackets and waistcoats were often

Late Victorian rural clothing continued into the Edwardian era. These haymakers, photographed in the early 1900s, wear wide-brimmed straw hats or cloth caps, their shirt sleeves rolled up, and their corduroy trousers tied under the knees.

discarded, as before, and shirt sleeves were rolled up, although removing the shirt was still considered indecent. Dungaree-style work overalls came into use during the 1930s, although some older men, mainly shepherds, wore traditional smocks until these finally died out with the last generation of wearers between the world wars. Wide-brimmed straw or felt hats were still worn in the Edwardian era, but later hat brims generally grew smaller and many farm labourers adopted the cloth cap that, by the turn of the century, had become a popular style with working men.

WOMEN

Like men, female agricultural workers wore practical clothing when toiling outdoors, keeping a better outfit for church on Sundays and for holidays. In the Georgian and Regency eras basic workwear typically comprised a thick woollen or flannel gown in winter and lighter calico or linen in summer, the hemline worn above the ankles. A popular choice was the 'bedgown', a casual three-quarter-length wraparound overdress often left open below the waist and draped up to reveal a coloured petticoat, while another characteristic working garment was the shorter bodice or jacket, worn with a stout petticoat. Both styles were teamed with a white or coloured half-apron tied around the waist, and a plain, checked or striped linen kerchief folded over the shoulders, its points tied or tucked in at the front. Traditionally, heads were covered with a white mob cap and often topped with a felt hat in winter or a wide-brimmed straw hat in summer. Another rural style, popular from Scotland to Hampshire and Sussex, was a round bonnet with fabric hood gathered on to a cane brim, called an 'ugly'; effectively shielding the eyes from glare and protecting the face from sunburn, this later evolved into the Victorian sun bonnet.

For extra warmth a large woollen cloak or a shawl was worn, the hooded red cloak familiar from the folk tale *Little Red Riding Hood* being closely associated with English countrywomen in the eighteenth and early nineteenth centuries. Some regions had local variants, such as the fringed woollen shawls worn in Somerset, Devon and

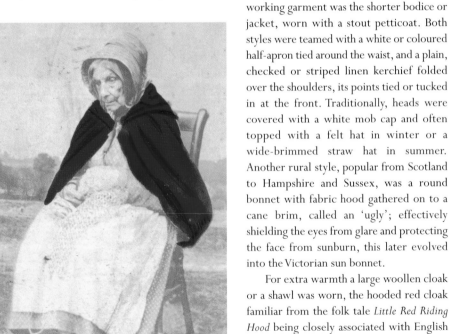

A Bedfordshire centenarian, photographed in the 1870s, wears a print dress, apron, bonnet, and an old-fashioned hooded red cloak, formerly associated with English countrywomen.

Cornwall, called 'whittles' or 'West Country rockets'. Similar to these were the long blue cloaks worn by Welsh countrywomen, with blue or striped flannel petticoats, brown bedgowns and men's beaver hats. Tourists visiting Wales noticed that local women went bare-legged or wore footless stockings, similar footless 'huggers' being reported in rural Scotland. A lack of stockings and shoes signified poverty. Northern England was also relatively poor until the end of the eighteenth century, and there women commonly wore nailed wooden clogs with leather uppers. Regular dress was also modified for certain tasks: for example, aprons were hitched up sideways for easier movement, and canvas oversleeves were often worn for haymaking. Country people did not stand on ceremony and in summer some women removed their outer clothes, working in the fields in a coloured petticoat pinned up between the legs, only a kerchief and half-laced stays covering their linen shift.

During the Victorian era the traditional bedgown and working jacket became outmoded; more usual by mid-century was a dress fitted at the waist,

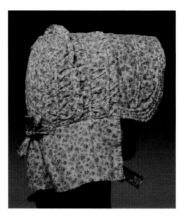

This sun bonnet from the Manx Museum, Isle of Man, is typical of the printed cotton or linen sun bonnets worn by female field workers throughout the nineteenth and early twentieth centuries.

East Sussex hop-picking families, c. 1900. Both children and adults are wearing regular dress with various hats, many using aprons to protect their clothes from hop-juice stains.

This clothing catalogue from Barkers of Kensington advertises a land-wear suit and brace-and-bib overalls for female farmworkers during the Second World War.

For the land ... for home .. emergency and every sort of practical wear—**THIS DEPARTMENT CATERS ECONOMICALLY!**

So marvellous are the values that their fame has spread through the length and breadth of the land! Compare these offers! Remember that the qualities are as sound and reliable AS ANY! Yet the prices—you'll notice—are actually money saving!

★ FOURTH FLOOR DISPLAY HALL

5/UL.1—LANDWEAR SUIT. Perfectly tailored, in heavy quality Corduroy Velveteen. In shades of Khaki, Fawn, Mole, Mid Brown and Dark Brown. Three-quarter length coat with tailored collar and revers—one ... and two patch ...

5/UL.2—Air Raid Emergency SUIT in warm woollen fabric in soft texture and strong wearing quality. Perfectly cut and perfect fitting. All in one-piece with zipper fastening up front and sash at waist. Two useful pockets ... In Shades of Navy, Black, ...

5/UL.4—White Drill Cross-Over OVERALLS. With long sleeves as illustrated, or with short sleeves. Perfectly tailor-made, especially for Barkers, in strong wearing and excellent Washing Drill. Roll collar to waist and sash tying at back. Sizes to fit 38, 40, 42 and 44 in. hips. Price **4/11**
Postage 4d.
In Shrunk Drill ... **5/11**
Heavier quality White Drill Crossover Overalls. Shrunk **7/11**
Superior quality Shrunk Drill. Price ... **8/11**
Also Cotton Casement Overalls, style and sizes as above. In shades of Navy, Butcher, Saxe, Brown, Bottle, Mid Green, Beige, Rose and Grey. Price ... **4/6**
Superior quality Linette, colours as above ... **6/11**
Outsize Overalls in all qualities. To fit 46in. hips ... **1/- ex.**
Postage 4d.
White Canteen Caps ... **1/6**
Postage 2d.

5/UL.5—Brace and Bib OVERALLS. Made in strong quality Drill. Well cut and excellent fitting and strongly sewn. Especially tailor-made for Barkers and with two useful pockets. In shades of Khaki, Navy and Mid Brown. Sizes to fit 38, 40, 42, 44in. hips. Price, each ... **8/11**
Postage 4d.
Same shape in Showerproof Gabardine in Khaki only. Sizes as above ... **10/6**

High St London W8 'Phone: Western 5432

The uniform of the first Women's Land Army, formed in 1917, comprised a belted knee-length overall coat, breeches, boots, gaiters and a felt hat. Most women would never have considered wearing breeches or trousers before the war.

worn without the fashionable supports of crinoline frame or, later, the bustle. These were often made of warm flannel or linsey-woolsey in winter, and plain, checked or striped cotton material in summer. Dresses were protected by a large apron, sometimes fashioned from sacks or sugar bags for heavy or dirty work. Coats and shawls were now common outer garments, the shawl still retained in rural areas well into the twentieth century. Sturdy boots or overshoes were usual for outdoors, rubber galoshes first appearing in the 1890s. A distinctive style of cotton sun bonnet with curtains of fabric protecting the neck was worn from around the mid-nineteenth century until at least the First World War in some areas. In *Lark Rise to Candleford* (1945), Flora Thompson painted a vivid picture of 1890s Oxfordshire female field workers:

> They worked in sun bonnets, hob-nailed boots and men's coats, with coarse aprons of sacking enveloping the lower part of their bodies. One ... was a pioneer of trousers; she sported a pair of her husband's corduroys; the others compromised with ends of old trouser legs worn as gaiters.

During the two world wars women took over much essential farm work. The Women's Land Army was formed in 1917; its uniform comprised a belted knee-length overall coat, breeches (scarcely worn by women before the war), boots, gaiters and a felt hat. In some areas leggings, clogs, jerseys and mackintoshes were also supplied in the summer and autumn of 1917. Following suit, other farming women gradually adopted breeches or trousers, or wore a more modern calf-length skirt with boots. A new Women's Land Army was created in 1939; standard-issue workwear during the Second World War included overall coats, mackintoshes, dungarees, rubber boots and sou'westers, although in practice a variety of clothes was worn, often a blouse or jersey with dungaree-style overalls and a headscarf. Some land girls from poorer backgrounds owned a better wartime wardrobe than they had ever had in civilian life.

This Second World War Women's Land Army girl wears her official uniform of shirt, green woollen jersey, brown cord knee breeches, long socks, brown lace-up shoes, and brown felt hat.

FISHING

MEN

The sea and fishing have always been integral to the working life of Britain, and early sources demonstrate close links between the clothing of ordinary sailors (who did not wear a regulation naval uniform until 1857) and that of fishermen, reflecting their shared working environment. The Georgian mariner's outfit might comprise a coarse linen shirt, striped waistcoat, coloured neckerchief, short jacket and loose canvas 'slops', formed either like wide knee breeches or the longer, loose trousers, garments that preceded by several decades the introduction of trousers into fashionable dress. Depictions of fishermen from the early nineteenth century show a motley assortment of plain and striped clothing, including short jackets and breeches or wide slops, sometimes worn with knee-length tarred aprons or petticoats on top, and with short or thigh-length leather boots. Headwear comprised a felt brimmed hat or a striped or red knitted stocking cap, a style known as both a 'brewer's cap' and a 'fisherman's cap' and worn for many years, even by twentieth-century yachtsmen.

As the nineteenth-century fishing industry developed, fishermen's clothing grew more functional. The term 'oilskin' was first recorded during the 1810s, meaning linen or cotton material brushed with boiled linseed oil to repel water. As oilskin increasingly replaced tarpaulin (tar-impregnated canvas), oilskin hats, trousers, jackets and coats became the preferred waterproof clothing for deep-sea fishermen, sailors and lifeboatmen when out in rough weather. By the 1840s and 1850s some seamen were beginning to wear brace-and-bib style dungarees or overalls, and practical oilskin sou'wester hats designed with an upturned brim, the lip of which channelled water backwards towards the long, slanting back brim, where it ran off, away from the wearer's neck, on to the oilskin coat. Besides waterproof oilskins, heavy woollen cloth 'fearnought' (or 'fearnaught') jackets were also worn by some fishermen – garments first used in the 1770s during Captain Cook's voyages.

From the 1860s onwards local photographs of fishing communities in Norfolk, Yorkshire, Sussex, Devon, Cornwall and elsewhere reveal that

Opposite:
This photograph from the Sutcliffe Collection, Whitby, portrays a typical late-Victorian fisherman wearing a sleeveless jerkin over the popular gansey sweater, with thick trousers, long knitted stockings, leather sea boots and an oilskin hat.

Fishermen at a capstan, illustrated in W. H. Pyne's *Costume of Great Britain* (1805), wear diverse, colourful garments including short jackets, wide 'slops', trousers, leather sea boots, and red fishermen's caps.

fishermen were wearing sturdy canvas trousers, either with a shirt-like garment cut like a short farm-labourer's smock, but made of canvas and also known as a 'slop', or the blue or grey fishermen's knitted sweater or 'gansey'. Sometimes a warm gansey was worn under a slop shirt, or a sleeveless jerkin was layered over the gansey. Thigh-high leather sea boots were usual, with long knitted stockings or footless leg warmers often worn over the trousers to line the heavy boots. Sea boots might be treated with goose fat or melted cod liver mixed with lard to keep them waterproof. Headwear ranged from the oilskin sou'wester, through bowlers and felt brimmed hats, to the tam-o'-shanter style bonnet popular in Scotland, and kepi-style peaked caps.

Early-twentieth-century fishermen continued to wear canvas trousers, thick socks or leg warmers, long sea boots, ganseys, and heavy-duty canvas shirts or slops, often with a white or coloured neckerchief. Over time, dungarees, thick pilot coats and yellow oilskins became common for outerwear, worn over the gansey, although, later on, water-resistant rubberised clothing offered an alternative to oilskin for overalls, coats and trousers, and rubber boots had largely replaced leather boots by the

Fishermen on Rye beach, East Sussex, 1842; by the mid-nineteenth century more functional protective sea clothing, such as the sou'wester oilskin hat, was beginning to develop.

1930s. For headwear, the skipper of an Edwardian fishing trawler might still formally don a respectable bowler hat when entering harbour, but otherwise fishing crews usually wore the sou'wester hat in foul weather, or the regular working man's cloth cap, a peaked cap or a knitted woollen hat.

THE FISHERMAN'S GANSEY

The garment most closely associated with fishermen is the knitted sweater called a 'jersey', 'Guernsey', or nowadays usually by its dialect name 'gansey'. Its origins may be traced to the late eighteenth century, to the Channel Islands, where worsted spinning and knitting were well established, and where it is thought the close-fitting garments knitted from worsted-spun yarn were first produced. In the early nineteenth century these comfortable garments, which we would today call 'jerseys', 'jumpers' or 'pullovers', were first called 'Guernsey jackets'; later in the nineteenth century they became popular throughout British coastal areas and acquired various regional names, such as 'knit frock', 'knitted frock', 'worsted frock' or 'Guernsey frock'. Essentially tubular in shape, with gussets under the arms and short slits at the sides for easy movement, ganseys also had a tight neck, welt and cuffs to keep out freezing winter winds. The hard twist given to the wool during spinning and the tightly knitted stitches, combined with the wool's natural oils, not only ensured that the gansey was warm and windproof, but also offered some protection against rain and sea spray.

Before mass-production and the wide availability of ready-made clothes, ganseys were hand-knitted, using long stocking needles. They were made in many fishing ports, from Scotland to Cornwall. Some fishermen knitted their own ganseys, although usually women and girls knitted for their menfolk, and the knitting of ganseys for sale became an important source of extra income for the community. Although the classic Guernsey pattern was plain, often designs were knitted across the chest, upper back and the top of the sleeves, the most elaborate ganseys being reserved for 'Sunday best'. Many fishing communities developed their own styles and complex patterns that were unique to their geographical region and often passed down from mother to daughter. Theoretically, it was therefore possible to identify the village or even the family that a gansey came from, if the wearer was tragically drowned, or if the garment was stolen. Inland boatmen, children and some fisherwomen also wore ganseys. Sturdy, hard-wearing garments, they often lasted for many years and might be passed down the generations.

Blue or grey hand-knitted ganseys were often ornamented with patterns across the chest and upper arms. This example survives in the Manx Museum, Isle of Man.

WOMEN

Hardy fisherwomen undertook some fishing and traditionally dug for cockles, mussels and other shellfish, netted shrimps, and helped with landing, preparing and selling fish. They were among the first females to wear distinctive occupational garments that bore little resemblance to respectable fashionable dress. In 1773 the novelist Fanny Burney, visiting Teignmouth in Devon, was shocked by the unconventional working outfits devised by local fisherwomen:

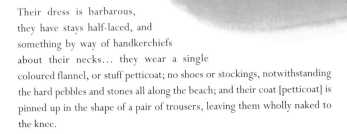

> Their dress is barbarous, they have stays half-laced, and something by way of handkerchiefs about their necks... they wear a single coloured flannel, or stuff petticoat; no shoes or stockings, notwithstanding the hard pebbles and stones all along the beach; and their coat [petticoat] is pinned up in the shape of a pair of trousers, leaving them wholly naked to the knee.

This female shrimper wears practical late-Georgian fisherwomen's clothing: a short petticoat with bare legs for wading, a sleeveless jacket-bodice, short-sleeved blouse and mob cap.

Genteel tourists visiting Britain's fishing villages and harbours expressed horror at, yet were fascinated by, fisherwomen's adoption of 'indecent' bifurcated garments and short skirts that revealed bare legs and feet, stockings and shoes usually being put on only when going to market. During the late-Georgian and Regency eras the usual linen cap and kerchief were often worn with a bedgown or jacket and short petticoat or improvised 'trousers' suited to wading in water. Local variations were also recorded: for example, a shrimp catcher on Hartlepool beach was depicted in 1819 wearing knee breeches under a hitched-up dress and a headscarf.

Clothing styles evolved over time, and the typical Victorian fisherwoman wore a calf-length or even knee-length plain or striped petticoat, a blouse or bodice with short sleeves or longer sleeves rolled up, a large apron, and a tartan or plain shawl that could be worn as a headscarf; she would have a basket strapped to her back or balanced on her head. Legs and feet might be left bare for wading, but more usual were dark stockings and flat leather shoes, sturdy boots, or occasionally clogs. Scottish fisher girls from Aberdeen

Opposite:
The Tenby Prawn Seller, by W. P. Frith, 1880, from the National Museum of Wales, shows the short skirt, apron and shawl worn by Welsh women who netted and carried shrimps to market. Stockings and boots were worn only for visiting town.

Newhaven (Edinburgh) fishwives often posed in their picturesque outfits for Victorian studio photographers. This fisherwoman wears a bold-striped flannel dress, folded apron, cloak and fringed shawl.

and Newhaven (near Edinburgh) working at English fishing ports were especially renowned for their distinctive outfits comprising brightly coloured blouses, fringed shawls wound around the neck or head, long cloaks, striped flannel skirts, and large aprons pinned up at the sides to form a deep pocket for carrying. Gaily dressed Newhaven fishwives often posed for souvenir studio photographs and postcards, until their traditional clothing was eventually replaced by more modern working garments. Their picturesque costume subsequently became preserved as a form of folk dress, worn by local women as late as the 1920s and 1930s for special occasions.

Remote or conservative coastal communities resisted change, and in some areas nineteenth-century customs persisted into the inter-war era. For example, during the 1930s Welsh cockle women from the Gower Peninsula would still ride out to the cockle beds at low tide on donkeys, wearing shawls secured around their heads with bands, short skirts, coarse dark stockings,

This postcard from the early twentieth century shows fisherwomen gathering bait wearing plain ankle- or calf-length skirts, chequered shawls, and headscarves – traditional dress still worn in some areas in the 1930s.

and rubber-soled flat shoes. Fashion eventually shifts, however, and technical innovations influenced fisherwomen's occupational dress. By the First World War younger women generally wore modern calf-length skirts with woollen sweaters, bibbed oilskin or rubberised aprons, and wellington boots. By the 1940s trousers, dungarees or overalls were common, the hair being secured in a headscarf.

Scottish fisher girls at Great Yarmouth c. 1915 wear more modern protective clothes, including oilskin or rubberised bibbed aprons and rubber boots.

DOMESTIC SERVICE

HISTORICALLY, noble and upper-class households retained numerous servants, while lower down the social scale small farmers and tradesmen usually employed one or two general servants. Domestic servants were generally better dressed than other workers since they lived and worked in closer proximity to the wealthy and fashionable, and they were also expected to demonstrate their employers' prosperity and status through their appearance. They often received cast-off clothes from their master or mistress, or had livery or other working garments provided. Diversity in servants' dress reflected the division of labour within the household and their social differences, expressing their position within the servant hierarchy.

MALE SERVANTS

Upper servants: butlers, valets and pages. In large households superior male servants (namely house stewards in prestigious establishments, butlers and valets) initially followed contemporary fashion, and in the Georgian era wore a frock coat, waistcoat, white shirt, knee breeches, stockings, buckled shoes, and usually a wig. By the turn of the nineteenth century wigs and hair powder were outdated, and during the 1810s trousers came into vogue: upper servants gradually adopted the new modes but sometimes lagged respectfully behind their masters, Regency valets typically wearing queue wigs, and butlers retaining old-fashioned knee breeches or pantaloons into the Victorian era, when a blue coat with velvet collar and metal buttons became usual for evening wear. Later, the butler's formal evening attire evolved into a dark tailcoat and trousers, white waistcoat, shirt and white bow tie, only his white gloves distinguishing him from his master. His daytime outfit typically comprised a dark or striped waistcoat, dark or pin-striped trousers, and often a black tie. These conventions continued into the twentieth century, the butler's conservative appearance conveying an air of old-fashioned dignity while regular menswear grew progressively casual.

Pages, rarer in our period than previously, were also considered upper servants. In the eighteenth century they often wore a form of livery, while

Opposite:
Maids of All Work,
1864–5, by John
Finnie, from the
Geffrye Museum,
London, portrays
mid-Victorian
housemaids
wearing
half-aprons
over grey dresses
supported by
the fashionable
crinoline frame.

This illustration from *Mrs Perkins's Ball* by W. M. Thackeray (1847) shows the butler, right, wearing the early-Victorian butler's evening outfit of velvet-collared tailcoat and old-fashioned knee breeches. The footman (centre) wears livery.

the Victorian page boy's uniform comprised a fitted waist-length jacket and slender pantaloons or long trousers, the padded jacket chest bearing rows of gilt buttons, inspiring the page's popular appellation – 'Buttons'. He also wore white gloves and a top hat, until the hat was replaced by a smaller pillbox cap from around 1890.

Lower servants and household livery. Prosperous families often provided special identifying livery for their lower male servants who were on public display. Richly braided livery suits tailored in the family colours, their heraldic crest embroidered on the coat, derived from medieval custom and were fashionable in the expanding cities of late-Georgian Britain. In his novel *Humphrey Clinker* (1771), Tobias Smollett described how country folk, 'seduced by the appearance of coxcombs in livery, ... swarm up to London in hopes of getting into service where they can live luxuriously and wear fine clothes.'

The Jealous Maids, an engraving by John Collet, 1772, depicts a Georgian footman wearing a brightly coloured household livery coat with contrasting lining and collar, and laced waistcoat.

In prosperous households numerous menservants, including footmen, coachmen, grooms, postilions, running footmen and porters, wore livery suits styled according to contemporary dress and comprising a frock coat, waistcoat, narrow breeches, stockings, buckled shoes, powdered wig, and a beaver hat, the coat collar and cuffs usually of a contrasting colour, and the garments typically ornamented with costly silver or gold lace. Sumptuously attired postilions were an important feature of the grander equipages, while the eighteenth century was also the heyday of the running footman, whose fanciful livery included a short braided jacket, broad, fringed waist sash, narrow breeches decorated with rosettes at the knees, white stockings, light pumps, and a tasselled or feathered velvet cap. Ostentatious, personalised servants' livery visibly expressed a family's wealth and social position and conveyed a sense of splendour precisely when fashionable gentlemen themselves were beginning to favour the simpler 'country' look of plain frock coat, riding breeches and leather boots.

A surviving footman's livery suit on display at Lanhydrock, Cornwall (National Trust), dating from 1904, includes eighteenth-century-style braided coat, waistcoat and plush breeches in the Tregoning family colours of blue and silver.

In some households elaborate livery was worn only between noon and early evening, during social visiting hours, or when guests were entertained; otherwise, footmen and other lower servants often wore plain frock coats when undertaking regular duties. They also received a set of practical work clothes, including linen smocks for footmen when powdering their masters' wigs, and sometimes coarse shirts and leather or stout cloth breeches. From the 1790s onwards it was mainly footmen who wore extravagant silver- or gold-braided coats, plush breeches, silk stockings and buckled shoes or pumps. In old families the livery colours were a long-established tradition, but the *nouveaux riches* often invented vivid colour schemes, creating garish outfits for their lower servants. By the turn of the century the colourful livery of lower servants had diverged significantly from regular fashion, becoming a picturesque, 'fossilised' costume resembling formal court dress.

Footmen. In the Regency era footmen's livery coats became narrower, cut away in style, and developed high collars, the employer's crest (if any) now relegated to the coat buttons. Powdered wigs persisted in some households well into the Victorian era, or were replaced by hair powder, the anachronistic tricorne or bicorne hat eventually being superseded by a silk top hat bearing a rosette-like cockade. Footmen also received practical work clothes that might include overall trousers, fustian or jean jackets, and leather and white aprons for different cleaning duties. From the mid-nineteenth century onwards the use of showy livery declined, being regarded increasingly as pretentious or in poor taste, although ornate Georgian-style

footmen's livery and wigs or hair powder were retained in the grander residences. Otherwise, between the 1860s and 1880s a dark brass-buttoned coat, or shortened 'coatee' and matching trousers became more usual for the well-dressed footman, along with a striped gold-yellow and black waistcoat and white cotton 'Berlin' gloves. By the early twentieth century a dark tailcoat, plain or striped waistcoat and white bow tie were usual for formal wear.

A formally dressed butler wearing a dark suit and white bow tie, with footmen in Georgian-style livery, outside their employer's imposing residence, c. 1904–7.

A household coachman poses in the studio wearing his livery of elegant frock coat, white buttoned breeches, and leather top boots. He carries a silk top hat bearing a cockade, his outer box coat draped over the chair.

Coachmen, grooms and stable boys.
Victorian household coachmen and stable staff generally wore a plainer livery suited to their occupation, although some coachmen had to wear extravagant laced coats and wigs for public show. The coachman's outer protective garment was a capacious greatcoat

that traditionally had a high collar and overlapping shoulder capes, this overcoat later being termed a 'box coat'. Beneath was worn an elegant double-breasted frock coat with tight-fitting white breeches and leather boots. As late as 1912, M. W. Webb wrote in *The Heritage of Dress* that modern coachmen 'wear the tall hat, the bright buttons, doeskin breeches and top boots characteristic of the … riding dress of the gentleman of the beginning of the 19th century'.

Coachmen also received practical working garments, for example overall-like smocks to cover their clothes when rubbing down the horses. Under-grooms and stable boys wore a loose brown jacket in the eighteenth century and, commonly, a fitted waist-length coatee, similar to the jockey's shirt, by the mid-nineteenth century. Victorian and early-twentieth-century grooms typically wore breeches or wide jodhpurs, with leggings, gaiters or top boots, white cravats and often a brightly coloured waistcoat.

This chauffeur, photographed c. 1903, models the early chauffeur's outfit of double-breasted tunic, breeches or jodhpurs, leather boots and gaiters, and peaked cap.

Chauffeurs. By the early twentieth century some prosperous families were acquiring motor cars. The first chauffeurs, in recognition of their equestrian heritage, typically wore riding breeches or jodhpurs and boots or gaiters, with a brass-buttoned jacket, a peaked cap and gauntlet gloves, also using a double-breasted outer coat in cold or wet weather. During the 1930s this early chauffeur's uniform was replaced by the more modern outfit of knee-length coat and regular trousers, only the peaked cap and leather driving gloves signifying their role.

General menservants. Modest households employing just one or two unclassified male servants did not supply livery, although provision of winter and summer clothing, apart from underwear and shoes, was usually part of the hiring agreement.

Household gardeners in the greenhouse at Mystole Park, Kent, have removed their jackets and wear starched collars and ties with the working man's cloth cap, c. 1900.

The conservative rural manservant might wear traditional knee breeches and stockings well beyond their fashionable life, and essentially clothing varied with duties, for the one man might function as groom and gardener in the morning and footman and butler later in the day. When serving indoors, a general manservant of the late nineteenth or early twentieth century usually dressed like the butler in larger houses: a formal jacket or tailcoat, dark trousers and a white apron for waiting at table.

FEMALE SERVANTS

Housekeepers. The head of the female servant hierarchy was the housekeeper, usually a mature woman who represented her mistress and supervised the housemaids; a large bunch of household keys hung from her waist, symbolising her authority. Early housekeepers generally wore a cap, neckerchief and apron, like other female servants, but these accessories were often discarded when they became outmoded and came to signify service in the mid-nineteenth century. The Victorian or Edwardian housekeeper's formal appearance distinguished her from her subordinates, her dress usually made in the prevailing style from sober black fabric, reflecting her status and responsible position. Younger housekeepers followed fashion, wearing shorter dresses from the 1910s onwards, although elderly housekeepers often favoured stately floor-length garments.

Georgian and Regency maidservants. In eighteenth- and early-nineteenth-century Britain female servants were numerous, but not always as visible as male servants. Although their wages were lower than men's, they were not issued with household livery, and were generally expected to buy their own working garments. Sometimes maids received hand-me-down clothing from their employers, however, and, since their workwear was not usually closely prescribed, many Georgian commentators complained that fashionably dressed female servants were easily mistaken for their mistresses. City maids were especially stylish, and an urban housekeeper or maid wearing a good gown, quilted petticoat, neat white apron, muslin kerchief and prettily trimmed day cap might conceivably resemble the lady of the house when dressed in informal indoor attire. Conversely, since servants' work garments generally reflected their employers' residence and status, the general maid-of-all-work in a humbler residence, or a country maidservant, might wear a basic petticoat that cleared her ankles,

The Maid of All Work's Prayer, 1801, by Thomas Rowlandson illustrates the typical late-Georgian housemaid's working outfit of plain, coloured washing gown, patterned kerchief, half-apron and mob cap.

with a jacket or longer bedgown, checked half-apron, colourful neckerchief and mob cap. In general, by the early nineteenth century a plain coloured or printed calico or linen washing dress was considered appropriate, worn with a plain or patterned kerchief, a half-apron and mob cap. Since maids' clothing broadly followed fashion, waistlines rose and fell and caps altered shape to accommodate changing hairstyles.

Victorian housemaids. As the nineteenth century advanced, more females entered service, becoming chamber, parlour, kitchen, scullery or laundry maids in large households where roles were clearly defined, although many worked alone, or with just one or two others as general maids-of-all-work. By the early Victorian era a washable cotton dress was the usual working garment, often of plain grey or another coloured material, or occasionally tartan or striped fabric. Although maids' work dresses were often worn shorter than ladies' gowns, their style followed fashion, and some servants adopted the vast, impractical crinoline frame introduced in 1856.

Clothing varied slightly according to the task, and aprons were changed regularly between different duties, for example after cleaning the grates and before making beds. Linen caps usually contained the hair; the day cap was no longer a fashionable accessory and therefore became a symbol of service. In some households a custom evolved for maids to change from their morning workwear into more formal outfits for the afternoons, when they might be seen by visitors. As demand soared for female dining-room and drawing-room servants, and parlourmaids' tasks increasingly became footmen's duties, it became usual for maids to exchange their black stockings, coloured work dresses and coarse aprons after lunch for white stockings, a better-quality dark gown and white apron.

As servants' lives grew increasingly regulated, standardised outfits gradually developed for Victorian housemaids, uniforms that clearly demonstrated their subservient status. A black or dark dress was the usual uniform for parlour, chamber and 'in-between' maids, worn with starched white cuffs, apron and cap. Initially half-aprons were the norm, but during the 1880s aprons acquired a bib, while after mid-decade white caps grew tall in

Two maids pose for a photograph in the late 1890s, wearing formal afternoon uniforms of black dress, starched white collar and cuffs, bibbed apron, and neat cap with streamers.

Right: This
parlourmaid
poses in the
photographer's
studio c. 1886–90,
wearing her
domestic servant's
formal uniform
of black dress,
newly introduced
bibbed apron and
fashionable
tall cap.

Far right: This
housemaid to an
Edinburgh family
was photographed
in the early 1910s.
The V-shape of her
apron is typical of
the late-Victorian
and Edwardian eras.

shape, following fashion. During the 1890s formal uniforms became more frivolous, dresses fashioned with puffed 'leg-o'-mutton' sleeves, the apron bib developing frills and shoulder straps, and the cap now a pert 'pom-pom' headdress fastened on top of the head, worn with long streamers for afternoons. In the twentieth century various work garments were worn in the mornings, such as a plain or print dress and the outmoded mob cap, but maids' afternoon uniforms continually evolved: dainty caps were worn far back on the head; smaller aprons developed a narrow V-shaped bib during the early 1900s; and dress hemlines grew shorter during the 1910s. By the inter-war era hemlines had risen to just below the knee, and uniforms were often made from blue or green rayon.

Ladies' maids. A lady's personal maid, ideally a young woman, was expected to dress neatly and was generally of fashionable appearance, since her duties included handling fine clothing, and she was usually first to receive her mistress's cast-offs. Nonetheless, the lady's maid in a large household usually wore a white cap and apron with her dress, like other maidservants.

Kitchen staff. The cook and her kitchen and scullery maids, who were not usually seen above stairs, generally wore plain or printed cotton dresses with short sleeves, or donned washable protective sleeves and coarse aprons for cooking or rough work. An overall covering the whole dress might be worn by Victorian and Edwardian cooks, but strictly in the kitchen.

Nannies and nursery maids.
Like other maids, nannies and nursery maids traditionally wore fashionable dress, with an apron and cap. During the Victorian era they too developed a uniform of a plain dress worn with a white apron and cap. In *Household Management* (1861), Mrs Beeton recommended grey for nannies, and in the early twentieth century the Astors' nanny at Cliveden, Buckinghamshire, still wore a white blouse and grey skirt in the mornings, and a dark grey dress for afternoons. Others generally wore a black or dark dress,

George Cruikshank's illustration for *The Greatest Plague of Life* (1847) shows domestic servants, including the cook, left, whose rolled-up sleeves express her kitchen role.

although nannies trained at the prestigious Norland College (established 1892) were instantly recognisable by their light brown uniform and embroidered 'N' motif. When worn with an outdoor cape, starched cap and bibbed apron, the uniform of the late-Victorian and Edwardian nanny resembled that of nurses.

This photograph of the first Norland-trained nannies, 1892, shows their distinctive brown uniforms, devised to set them apart from other household servants when they began work.

L & N·W·R - N⁰ 9

PASSENGERS

LUGGAGE VAN

L & N · W · R · C

H. alken.

TRANSPORT

CANAL WORKERS

From the mid-eighteenth to the early twentieth century Britain's inland waterways provided an efficient method of carrying raw materials for industry and finished goods to market by boat. Most canal boats were owned by carrying companies, and initially were operated by teams of men whose families lived ashore. Early boatmen wore a version of the regular suit but often favoured a short working jacket (as opposed to the longer coat), or went without, their shirts teamed with open waistcoats, breeches, coarse stockings, and stout hobnail leather boots, while some adopted loose smocks. By the mid-nineteenth century canal transport was facing competition from the railways, and the slashing of wages led to boatmen's families moving into the boats, where they lived and worked together in cramped and, inevitably, insanitary conditions. Boatmen typically wore heavy-duty corduroy or moleskin trousers with sturdy boots, shirts and waistcoats, or slop-type smocks or knitted jerseys, and in winter warm pea-jackets or thick blanket coats, while boatwomen adopted plain dresses, their earlier kerchiefs developing into shawls, and mob caps evolving into bonnets with a frill extending behind.

Following the campaigns of George Smith, who investigated and reported on the living and working conditions of canal workers, Canal Boats Acts were passed in 1877 and 1884. Gradually, as living standards improved and a sense of occupational pride returned, the unique culture of the canal people was revived and celebrated in music, gaily painted boats and bright costumes, customs now regarded as expressions of a 'traditional' lifestyle. Thus inspired, by the 1890s some canal companies were supplying standard outfits to their boatmen, including corduroy trousers, leather belts, velvet-collared jackets, brass-buttoned waistcoats, striped shirts, coloured neckerchiefs and braided braces. Other boatmen wore similar corduroy or moleskin trousers, striped and embroidered shirts, and bright neckerchiefs, the ornamentation of their clothes distinguishing them from other labourers, for canal women embroidered decorative braces and belts for the men in

Opposite:
This train guard from the London & North Western Railway, illustrated by Henry Alken in 1852, wears a smart dark-green company livery uniform with a peaked cap and buckled shoulder belt and pouch.

unique designs, and plaited multi-coloured wool braces.

By the 1890s boatwomen's dress was also colourful and recognisable: blouses were striped or floral-patterned, ankle-length striped skirts were often hemmed with contrasting bands, and shawls were generally crocheted or woven in grey, black and white plaid. Most prominent was the boatwoman's large bonnet, which, evolving during the nineteenth century, gave protection from rain and sun: this had a stiffened, quilted brim and a long 'curtain' of fabric falling over the shoulders, sometimes decorated with crochet lace, bows and streamers. Although younger boatwomen wore modern garments and hats by the First World War, some older females retained their traditional dress until the 1920s and 1930s.

This illustration from *Life of the Upper Thames* (1875) shows a narrowboat girl wearing a plain dress, and the boatwoman's distinctive bonnet with large fabric 'curtain'.

HORSE-DRAWN COACH AND CAB DRIVERS

In the late eighteenth century horse-drawn stage and mail coaches were the fastest method of road travel. Georgian coachmen wore a frock coat of hard-wearing fustian or similar material, breeches, leather boots, a sturdy caped greatcoat, and a round or tricorne hat, often trimmed with gold lace. Horse-drawn cabs (cabriolets), licensed by the authorities, appeared in 1823, and early cabmen wore the caped greatcoat, a wide-brimmed slouch hat, jockey boots and a brightly coloured neckerchief. From 1838 it became obligatory for all public-service vehicle drivers to wear an enamelled PSV (Public Service Vehicle) licence badge, and cabbies' badges were suspended around the neck or attached to clothing. By the mid-nineteenth century the typical cab driver's outfit was a caped greatcoat and a top hat or dome-shaped 'Bollinger', an early form of bowler; when not wearing the greatcoat, he wore a short jacket or a sleeved waistcoat, his legs often covered by a rug. Drivers of fast hansom cabs, who expertly negotiated busy Victorian city streets, were well-known for their dandified appearance in stylish coats, short capes, trousers, boots, top hat and gloves. By the century's close dark suits were usually worn, with a coat and bowler or other felt hat in winter, and sometimes a straw boater in summer.

BUS DRIVERS AND CONDUCTORS

Horse-drawn omnibuses were introduced during the 1820s, and early drivers typically wore a caped or plain coat, and a laced hat or peaked cap, their

The driver of a horse-drawn bus wearing a bowler hat and the usual driver's rug, 1902. The conductor wears a regular lounge suit.

conductors usually sporting a short jacket and trousers. No standard uniform existed for most omnibus crews throughout the horse-drawn era, so their PSV licence badges were essential for identifying them to the police and general public. The dress of Victorian bus crews broadly followed fashion, and by the mid-nineteenth century drivers usually wore a top hat with a coat, trousers and often a rug, the conductor also wearing a top hat. From the 1860s onwards the shorter morning coat and newly fashionable bowler hat became popular, especially with conductors, the lower bowler crown being more convenient for leaning inside to collect passengers' fares or announce stops.

Public Service Vehicle Licence badges were a legal requirement from 1838. These enamelled bus driver and conductor licence badges are early Victorian.

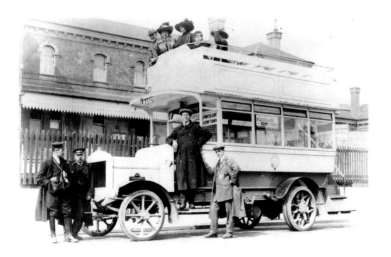

The crews of two Brighton motor buses, c. 1910–13, wearing double-breasted winter coats and peaked caps or cloth caps. The conductors on the outside both wear Bell Punch ticket machines.

Above: London Transport woman's peaked cap dating from the Second World War.

Right: A Portsmouth bus company employee, photographed in 1942, wears her regulation cap, coat and trousers. Note her prominent PSV bus driver's badge.

Far right: A London Transport 'clippie' (bus conductress) wears a Second World War uniform of white summer coat and peaked cap, 1940.

Money satchels were first used by bus conductors in around the 1880s, and the Bell Punch ticket machine by the 1890s, both probably introduced from tramcars. Only Metropolitan Railway horse-drawn bus conductors were issued with a uniform, this comprising a frock coat with metal buttons and peaked cap.

Motor buses became a viable alternative to horse power in the early 1900s, and some early motor-bus drivers, influenced by the dress of private motor-car chauffeurs, wore a double-breasted jacket with breeches, leather boots or gaiters, and a peaked cap. The traditional driver's rug being impractical with a mechanical vehicle, long double-breasted leather or woollen coats were used in winter, and white dustcoats in summer. During the 1910s bus crews gradually acquired recognisable uniforms comprising dark blue suits, and peaked caps bearing the bus company's badge. Female conductors employed during the First World War received seasonal uniforms: for example, the London General Omnibus Company winter outfit was a blue calf-length skirt, belted jacket with white piping, and a felt slouch hat; the summer uniform a white dustcoat and straw hat. Between the wars a lapelled jacket, based on the civilian lounge jacket, and smartly creased trousers became usual for men, with a dark winter overcoat and a shorter white summer coat and white rain-cover for the cap. When women joined the buses again during the Second World War, their uniform was grey and included trousers. Lightweight grey jackets with coloured collars were also popular for busmen's summer wear by the 1940s.

TRAM CREWS

During the 1860s and 1870s horse-drawn tramcars were introduced, early tram drivers wearing the customary frock coat and top hat of the era. Generally, by the 1870s a shorter morning coat or jacket and bowler hat were more common, many drivers continuing to wear smart civilian garments, and in winter an overcoat and large apron or rug wrapped high around the chest, like horse-drawn cab drivers. From the outset, some tram conductors wore neat kepi-style peaked caps bearing the company's badge, and, in time, brass-buttoned jackets, their leather money satchels and Bell Punch ticket machines, introduced by the 1880s, adding a businesslike air. Although some tram companies issued uniforms and insignia to their staff, many never developed a recognisable uniform during the horse-drawn era.

By the turn of the century electric tramcars were replacing

horse-powered trams, although old and new co-existed for some years. Local tram companies were also being taken over by municipal authorities, and the combination of modern vehicles and the desire for an identifiable city corporation image inspired the development of standardised uniforms for staff operating the new trams. The first electric-tram drivers, now called 'motormen', and their conductors typically wore the kepi cap with a quasi-military tunic, the cap bearing the local corporation badge or a brass badge with 'Conductor' or 'Motorman' written in script lettering. Soon the peaked cap grew larger, and many tram crews adopted smart hip-length tunics with a high collar, leather cuffs and parallel rows of large buttons, echoing the chauffeur's tunic: the buttons often bore the corporation's insignia, and the collar its initials and the wearer's employee number. Seasonal uniforms included a white cap rain-cover for summer, and for winter a warm double-breasted overcoat, worn by motormen with leather gloves. During the First World War women worked as tram conductors, and in some cities as drivers: their uniforms comprised a belted cloth jacket, a calf-length flared skirt and

Most tram companies issued uniforms only in the electric era. This Edwardian tram crew from Wigan wear quasi-military tunics and kepi caps.

Above: Uniforms were considered important for identifying early-twentieth-century municipal authority employees. This tram uniform button bears the insignia of the Belfast Corporation Tramways.

Above middle: A 1920s Derby tram crew wear smart double-breasted, metal-buttoned tunics, and peaked caps bearing their titles, 'Motorman' (driver) and 'Conductor', in metal letters.

Above right: This First World War tram conductress wears the Glasgow Corporation Tramways' unique female uniform of belted military-style tunic and tartan skirt.

a hat, with certain regional variations. For men, civilian-style lapelled jackets were usual by the later 1930s and 1940s, and during the Second World War those tramways still operating employed all-female crews who wore military-style cloth jackets and tailored skirts or trousers.

RAILWAY WORKERS

The first steam-hauled public railway, the Stockton & Darlington, opened in 1825. Early lines were operated by independent companies, and their engine crews wore a regular frock coat, or a cutaway dress coat, or a short, practical jacket, with trousers and a tall top hat. As scattered local lines expanded into a larger railway network, some companies provided identifying livery-style clothing for their drivers and firemen, beginning with the Sheffield, Ashton-under-Lyne & Manchester Railway, which in 1841 introduced a dark green cloth uniform with red edging. Similarly, by 1848 Great Western Railway engine crews were wearing blue trousers, white shirts, black neck cloths and peaked blue caps, the dark blue peaked cap from then onwards becoming standard wear for drivers. By the end of the century a regular uniform of jacket, trousers and cap had evolved for engine crews, with oilskins or warm pilot coats for bad weather, and for summer the comfortable working man's lightweight slop jacket.

Stationmasters, train guards and ticket collectors, who dealt with the public, typically wore the finest livery uniforms. During the 1850s and 1860s, mulberry, dark green or red double-breasted frock coats were popular; the collars, cuffs and caps of uniforms were often edged with gold or silver lace, and caps had a glazed peak, the outfit completed with a buckled shoulder belt and pouch. Porters generally received practical sleeved waistcoats or jackets and trousers in the company's colours: for example, Great Western Railway porters wore short green jackets with corduroy trousers, their jacket sleeves and black caps bearing the letters 'GWR'. Uniforms were worn with pride and signified employees' loyalty to the railway that provided them, while companies well understood the beneficial effect of smart working attire on staff morale and efficiency. Following the general trend towards sobriety in male dress, at the close of the nineteenth century the typical platform worker wore a dark frock coat or jacket, waistcoat, shirt, collar and tie, trousers, boots and peaked cap.

During the early twentieth century, main-line railway companies published complex uniform regulations covering all grades of staff, from stationmaster to lavatory attendant, specifying styles of garments and quality of cloth according to the employee's position and duties. In 1923 most companies were amalgamated into four major public railways, whose workers were expected to represent the corporate image. The GWR livery typified early-twentieth-century railway company uniforms. Their first-class stationmasters wore dark blue beaver overcoats, blue frock coats, and matching waistcoats and trousers, the coat borders and cuffs and the peaked caps ornamented with gold braid and bearing the GWR badge. Guards wore overcoats with GWR buttons and dark blue jackets, the word 'Guard' stitched in gilt thread beside the collar. Porters were issued with blue jackets with 'Porter' written on the collar and a number badge on the sleeve, or a blue serge vest (waistcoat) with linen sleeves. Some of these features continued for decades: for example, porters' linen-sleeved waistcoats were still worn in the 1970s. During the early twentieth century, like many other manual workers, engine crews adopted dungaree-style overalls and wore a peaked cap bearing the company's badge, or unofficially the working man's cloth cap.

This young railway worker from the Cheshire Lines Railway, photographed in the 1890s, wears the company's uniform and the peaked cap bearing its metal badge.

Many of these Cheshire Lines Railway employees, photographed c. 1900–10, wear the company's peaked caps, while others, including the engine driver, wear regular cloth caps.

PUBLIC SERVICE

This fireman of 1805 wears the bright livery uniform and arm badge of independent fire insurance companies. Their knee protectors and leather helmets were early forms of protective gear.

FIREFIGHTERS

The first fire brigades were part-time firemen employed by individual fire insurance companies following the Great Fire of London (1666). Understanding the value of a distinctive uniform to foster *esprit de corps* and promote their public image, several insurance companies were issuing their men with livery by the eighteenth century: caps, coats, waistcoats and breeches broadly followed fashion, but were made in a specified colour such as blue, green or crimson. A prominent silver badge was worn on the left arm to identify the company, an important emblem that came to symbolise the integrity of both wearer and insurance company. By the late eighteenth century some firemen were also adopting a leather helmet with a crest and a wide brim extending to a neck-flap at the back, an early example of protective work gear.

Early-nineteenth-century illustrations depict insurance company fire crews wearing brightly coloured livery suits with stockings, garters and leather top boots, but major changes occurred when independent brigades came under centralised control. James Braidwood, superintendent of the first combined brigade, the Edinburgh Fire Engine Establishment, formed in 1824, introduced a sober, more functional uniform for his organisation:

The whole are dressed in blue jackets, canvas trousers, and hardened leather helmets, having hollow leather crests over the crown to ward off falling materials. The form of this helmet was taken from the war helmet of the New Zealanders, with the addition of the hind flap of leather to prevent burning matter, melted lead, water, or rubbish getting into the neck of the wearer.

Following suit, in 1833 the main metropolitan insurance companies merged to form the London Fire Engine Establishment, after which individual company uniforms were discontinued, and crews were provided with plain grey coats and trousers and black leather helmets.

During the Victorian era further volunteer brigades were formed by railway companies, factories and other workplaces, their uniforms broadly following those of the fire engine establishments, with some variations. In 1866 the London Fire Engine Establishment became the Metropolitan Fire Brigade, and its leader, Massey Shaw, introduced the impressive brass crested helmet of the Parisian Sapeurs-Pompiers. Many provincial brigades adopted the new crested helmets with their front peak and back flap, some using leather versions with metal fittings. The Victorian fireman's uniform also included a single- or double-breasted tunic, worn with matching trousers tailored from densely woven Melton cloth. Tunic buttons were often ornamented with crossed hatchets and a helmet or torch, although some brigades used specially designed buttons, while a cloth badge denoting the brigade was displayed on the breast or arm. Blue and green uniforms were worn until the 1880s, when dark blue became standard, volunteer firemen often displaying coloured flashes on their tunic collars. The uniform was completed with high leather wellington boots, and a broad leather waist belt with a square brass buckle.

The early-twentieth-century firemen's uniform retained many Victorian features, including the dark blue metal-buttoned tunic, and the stout leather belt supporting pouches containing a hand axe, searchlight and other equipment. Waterproof mackintoshes and leggings, oilskin or rubberised

A volunteer fire crew from the Bishopstoke Fire Brigade, Hampshire, 1888, wear the dark tunics and crested metal helmets introduced in the mid-nineteenth century.

41

This crested Merryweather helmet of nickel-plated brass is thought to have been worn by a senior Brighton fire officer c. 1900.

These firemen, believed to be from Horsham, West Sussex, wear their smart dress uniforms for an official function, in the 1930s.

trousers, and rubber boots, available since the late nineteenth century, eventually came into regular use. Beginning in the mid-1930s, the traditional crested 'Merryweather' helmet was superseded by the black 'Cromwell' helmet; made of compressed cork, this type remained standard for years. The Auxiliary Fire Service was formed in 1938 in anticipation of war, and male recruits received uniforms, waterproof leggings, rubber boots, and military-style steel helmets. Women also joined the brigade, as watchers, drivers and despatch riders; their uniform was a navy woollen suit including a skirt or trousers, a soft fabric peaked cap, and a steel helmet.

POLICE OFFICERS

In the Georgian period constables and watchmen were responsible for patrolling the streets. In 1800 the Glasgow Police Act established Britain's first organised police force, its watchmen wearing long brown coats, their personal numbers painted on their backs. In 1805 members of the Bow Street Horse Patrol, the famous London watch, adopted blue coats and red waistcoats, followed by similar garments for the Foot Patrol in 1822. Sir Robert Peel's act of 1829 established the Metropolitan Police Force to combat crime in London, the earlier successes of the Bow Street patrols, recognisable in their red and blue outfits, having confirmed the value of a structured, uniformed organisation. However, public opinion was strongly against any kind of uniformed paramilitary corps, and accordingly the dress devised for the new 'Peelers' lacked any military connotations. Comprising a blue swallow-tailed coat, blue or white trousers according to the season, and a tall black top hat, the early policeman's outfit resembled regular male dress, except for a striped duty armlet on the left cuff of constables' coats, introduced in 1830, and white stitching on the collar indicating the wearer's division and personal number.

A significant new look for Metropolitan policemen developed in 1864, when outmoded tailcoats and civilian top hats were replaced by more functional tunics, knee-length greatcoats, and continental-style quasi-military helmets deriving from the German *Pickelhaube*. The high-collared, thigh-length tunics were belted, and a truncheon case was suspended from the belt, while metal numerals replaced the earlier embroidered collar numbers. The new sturdy, yet lightweight cork helmet, sometimes termed the 'custodian helmet', bore a plate displaying the divisional letter and number. Simultaneously, rank chevrons were introduced for sergeants, and their striped duty armlet, earlier worn on the right arm, shifted to the left. Provincial police forces essentially adopted the Metropolitan uniform, although regional variations existed: for example, in Kent a peaked shako-style cap was worn until 1897, while other forces wore variants of the regular helmet, some crowned with a small ridge or crest, others a spike. Equipment also grew more advanced, the rattle being replaced by a whistle in 1884, and a new truncheon was introduced in 1887, special truncheon pockets being fitted into trousers and greatcoats.

The basic police uniform established in the 1860s changed little for decades, although during the early twentieth century the tunic grew progressively shorter and slimmer in cut, and finally, during the 1940s, the Metropolitan Police introduced a civilian-style jacket.

Below left:
This humorous print of c. 1830 depicts a policeman wearing the early London Peelers' uniform of blue swallow-tailed coat and trousers and black top hat.

Below:
This policeman from Beith in Ayrshire, Scotland, photographed c. 1886, wears the functional tunic and continental-style helmet developed during the 1860s.

Right: This police officer, photographed in the early 1900s, wears the front-buttoning belted Victorian tunic that changed little for decades.

Far right: This Liverpool police constable wears a regulation tunic and crested helmet, 1936.

Right: This member of the Women's Auxiliary Police Corps wears a Second World War uniform of tailored jacket with metal buttons and a peaked cap, 1944.

Women played a minor role in the police force until the Second World War, when the Women's Auxiliary Police Corps was established. Uniforms for recruits working indoors comprised blue cotton overalls, with an armlet or breast badge bearing the letters 'WAPC', while female drivers wore tailored jackets with metal buttons, and skirt or trousers, with a peaked cap and gauntlet gloves.

POSTAL WORKERS

By the eighteenth century red was established as the colour of the British Postal Service; red was the royal colour of England, and the Georgian Post Office had its origins in royal couriers. In 1784 mail coaches were introduced. The guard protecting the mail and passengers inside the coach wore a gold-braided scarlet coat; he was armed and carried a bugle to announce the fast-approaching vehicle. In 1793 the Post Office issued London mail-coach guards and drivers with new scarlet cloth coats faced with blue lapels and linings, blue waistcoats, and black beaver hats.

Earlier, in 1772, the General Post Office had established an extensive network of letter carriers to make free house-to-house deliveries (the forerunners of our postmen), and in 1793 they too received smart uniforms comprising scarlet cutaway coats with blue lapels and cuffs, the brass

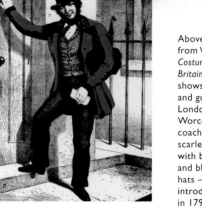

coat buttons inscribed with the wearer's unique number. Blue cloth waistcoats and black beaver hats with a gold hat band and cockade were also provided, but carriers had to supply their own breeches and, later, trousers.

The adoption of standardised garments outside London was slow, and provincial letter-carriers were not all issued with uniforms until 1834. Then, following wider uniform trends, the Victorian postman's uniform was redesigned. In 1855 a scarlet skirted frock coat replaced the tailcoat, with the carrier's number now worn on the collar, while the beaver hat gave way to a glazed top hat. Waterproof capes were also issued for protection, but nonetheless scarlet clothing quickly became dirty, and in 1861 the uniform was reversed, becoming a blue frock coat with scarlet collar and cuffs, the initials 'GPO' embroidered in white on the collar, and scarlet piping edging the blue waistcoat and outside trouser seams. In 1862 a shako cap, covered in blue cloth with red piping and a glazed peak, superseded the top hat, and in 1868 a shorter, military-style tunic replaced the frock coat and waistcoat, this uniform continuing until 1910.

Above: This scene from W. H. Pyne's *Costume of Great Britain* (1805) shows the driver and guard of the London to Worcester mail coach wearing scarlet cloth coats with blue lapels and black beaver hats – uniforms introduced in 1793.

Left: This song-sheet cover, 'The Postman's Knock' (1855–6), portrays a postman wearing the new uniform of scarlet skirted frock coat and glazed top hat.

Female postal workers model the Second World War uniform, c. 1941. In that year trousers were introduced and these slouch hats began to be replaced by peaked caps.

By the early 1900s the Post Office employed thousands of workers and took its uniforms seriously. In 1910 the Committee on Uniforms declared six grades of workers to be entitled to uniforms, including officers, postmen and women, mail-cart drivers and telegram messengers, ending distinctions between London and elsewhere. Simultaneously the tunic was replaced with a modern civilian-style lounge jacket, and in 1932 the shako helmet began to be phased out in favour of a peaked cap.

Although women had worked as letter carriers since the eighteenth century, the first female uniform items, a waterproof cape and skirt, were introduced only in 1894. During the First World War women were issued with a blue serge skirt, blue coat and blue straw hat, these hats being superseded in 1929 by felt slouch hats. Further changes accompanied the Second World War, the slouch hat being replaced by a peaked cap from 1941, and trousers being introduced for postwomen the same year.

HOSPITAL STAFF

During the eighteenth century the first hospitals serving only medical needs were established. Georgian surgeons wore regular dress but sometimes removed their coat and wig and donned a cap, apron and protective sleeves before an operation. Such practices were not, however, compulsory, and, although Victorian surgeons might use a bibbed apron and oversleeves, many performed operations wearing their street clothes, with no special garments protecting themselves or the patient. In 1889–90 rubber gloves were introduced for surgery, chiefly to protect surgeons' hands from the carbolic acid used to immerse the instruments. Soon afterwards a white coat began to be used by both male and female surgical staff, and at the turn of the twentieth century, following the recommendations of Joseph Lister, Scottish professor of surgery, sterilised theatre outfits came to be considered essential, forerunners of the modern operating gown, cap, rubber gloves, overshoes and face mask.

Nurses from Southampton Hospital, 1916, wear hygienic uniforms of coloured dresses with starched white caps, collars, aprons and detachable protective oversleeves.

Nurses' uniforms changed relatively little during the early twentieth century but hemlines rose to just below the knee, as seen in this photograph of a St Andrews nurse, 1940.

Initially most hospital nurses wore ordinary working dress with an apron and mob cap, and as late as 1858 Guy's Hospital nurses were identified chiefly by a round tin medal worn around the neck, inscribed with the wearer's position and ward. However, the growing trend was towards standardised garments for hospital nurses, fashioned in specific colours that identified the hospital and the different ranks within their occupation. Nurses began as probationers and were recognisable from their novice uniforms, the colour of their dresses and materials changing as they passed exams, advancing to become staff nurses and eventually sisters. For example, in 1895 probationers at the Middlesex Hospital wore black, grey or sombre-coloured cotton gowns, progressing to blue cambric or grey gingham dresses as nurses, and finally to violet serge dresses as sisters.

Essentially, nurses' outfits followed the fashionable style, but the starched white apron, cap, collar and cuffs created an efficient uniform that defined their role. A hospital matron was always identifiable by her appearance: often she wore a smart black gown with a white cap, but no apron. Nurses' apron and cap styles evolved over time, the late-Victorian apron gaining a bibbed front, and headdresses varying between nurses of different ranks and between hospitals. Initially dresses were often made of dark wool or worsted fabrics, including serge, zephyr and alpaca, which, being unwashable, were impractical: not until the early twentieth century was hygiene considered more important, and lightweight washable dresses were preferred. Hemlines rose gradually during the early twentieth century, ending just below the knee by the 1940s.

INDUSTRY AND MANUFACTURING

MINERS

The mining of iron, lead, tin and coal were all important to British industry throughout the period of this book. Late-Georgian illustrations depict northern colliers working on the surface wearing the usual working man's jacket or waistcoat and breeches, shoes, stockings and a hat or cap, and some also aprons. During the 1810s Welsh miners developed a unique suit for working underground, comprising a thigh-length smock frock, trousers and a pillbox-style hat, the garments thickly padded for protection from knocks, and giving some comfort when kneeling. Women and children also worked in the mines, the Children's Employment Commission's report of 1842 shocking the general public with its descriptions of working conditions. It revealed how women worked underground wearing only shifts or men's breeches or breeched skirts, and that teenage girls crawled through low tunnels pulling coal trucks, wearing ragged men's jackets and trousers, or flimsy shifts without stockings and shoes, or even going bare-breasted in half-shifts. Moreover, girls often laboured alongside men who wore only trousers or sometimes went completely naked in the stifling mines. Such 'immoral' practices caused an outcry and, following the report, women, girls and small boys were prohibited from working down the mines.

Boys aged ten and upwards and men continued to labour underground, usually wearing a coarse flannel shirt, or no shirt at all, with trousers sometimes padded after the Welsh style. By the late nineteenth century some miners were adopting rudimentary forms of protective workwear: for example, Cornish tin and lead miners wore boots with steel toecaps, and a compressed felt hat stiffened with pine resin, called a 'tull', although many miners resisted protective gear, considering it unmanly. Females now operated solely above ground, undertaking heavy work such as sorting coal and shifting tubs around the yard, and by the 1860s many pit-brow lasses throughout the North and Midlands were wearing padded trousers for warmth, easier movement and safety, since wide skirts could become caught on moving machinery or coal wagons. On top they wore a shift and waistcoat,

Opposite:
The Dinner Hour, Wigan, by Eyre Crowe, 1874, from Manchester City Art Gallery, depicts female textile millworkers wearing blouses, short skirts and protective pinafore dresses, with bare feet or wooden-soled clogs.

49

During the 1810s Welsh miners developed a thickly padded suit for working underground, comprising a thigh-length smock frock and trousers, worn with a pillbox-style hat, as shown in this engraving by R. Roffe after A. R. Blunt, 1819.

or commonly a hip-length smock frock, teamed with a thigh-length padded apron-like skirt, layered over the trousers. Headwear usually comprised a padded hood or linen cap topped with a scarf, and their feet were encased in sturdy clogs. Critics continued campaigning against trousers, and in some areas modest knee-length skirts were later worn on top; however, enlightened commentators saw the 'broo wenches' as bold pioneers of rational dress for women.

During the early twentieth century in the hotter mines some miners worked only in thin drawers, knee pads and clogs, but otherwise the typical miner of this era wore a shirt or sleeveless vest and trousers. Hard hats that protected the head from heavy blows became more common with increased use of cap lamps, but they were not compulsory, and some miners were still wearing soft cloth caps after the Second World War. Women continued working on the surface, some still championing trousers or breeches in the early twentieth century, while others wore blouses, shawls wound around their heads, and calf-length skirts and aprons of sacking, with thick stockings and clogs. By the 1940s younger pit-brow women wore practical, modern trousers, bringing female mining dress around full circle.

This 1870s photograph of a Wigan pit-brow girl demonstrates the kinds of unique protective clothes devised by Victorian female pit-head workers: a short frock worn over a padded apron-skirt and trousers, with a shawl, padded hood and reinforced boots.

NAVVIES

The term 'navvy', deriving from 'navigator', originally denoted labourers excavating canals for inland navigation, but later included men who built railways and roads. Early navvies wore knee breeches, shirts, waistcoats, and various caps and hats, their wide shirts often worn loose outside the breeches, like a short smock. By the Victorian era trousers of moleskin, corduroy and other stout materials were often rolled up to the shin and worn with sturdy, high-laced hobnail boots. In the mid-nineteenth century neckerchiefs and waistcoats were still brightly coloured, although many navvies worked without waistcoats, their shirt sleeves rolled up. Close-fitting stocking caps or brewers' caps were popular, and were often coloured or striped, as illustrated in the front cover image. By the late nineteenth century railway and road builders' clothes had become more sombre, following general trends in male dress. Navvies of this era and the early twentieth century wore plainer, dark waistcoats, and often tied their trousers below the knee, like agricultural workers.

BUILDERS

The building industry involved various trades, including brick-making, bricklaying and masonry. Georgian masons wore knee breeches, stockings and boots, with a shirt and waistcoat or short jacket, often with a half-apron and a felt hat. Both women and men participated in brick-making, women wearing the customary calf-length dress or petticoat and bedgown made with short sleeves, or with sleeves rolled up, teamed with a coarse apron, kerchief, and mob cap or felt hat. Builders generally discarded their jackets and worked in shirts or the sleeved waistcoats popular with many manual workers, and

In this scene from W. H. Pyne's *Costume of Great Britain* (1805), a female brick-worker wears a plain calf-length petticoat, ragged apron, sleeveless jacket-bodice and blouse, with her sleeves rolled up and a felt hat on her head.

This engraving from the *Book of English Trades* (1824) shows a bricklayer wearing trousers, a practical short jacket and bibbed apron, while his assistant below wears old-fashioned knee breeches.

Victorian builders wearing assorted slop jackets or their shirt sleeves, some using aprons and sturdy trousers tied below the knees. The photograph was taken in Peckham, London, c. 1880–90.

similar to the white flannel jackets often worn by builders' labourers. Some masons and bricklayers had adopted trousers by the 1820s, but others preferred old-fashioned knee breeches, for easier movement. In *Under the Greenwood Tree* (1872), Thomas Hardy described a mason of the 1840s:

he wore a long linen apron, reaching almost to his toes, corduroy breeches and gaiters, which, together with his boots, graduated in tints of whitish brown by friction against the lime and stone. He also wore a very stiff fustian coat … [whose] extremely large side pockets … bulged out … and as he was often engaged to work at buildings far away – his breakfast and dinners he carried in these pockets.

By the mid- to late-nineteenth century, builders' attire was essentially a version of the regular suit. Victorian photographs show trousers of corduroy and other hard-wearing materials, the knees often secured with string or straps. Some builders wore lounge jackets or loose white slop jackets; others wore waistcoats or only shirt sleeves, revealing their trouser braces. Masons and carpenters working in the building trade generally wore half-aprons or bibbed aprons, while headwear included various caps, bowlers and other felt styles. In the early twentieth century some builders adopted comfortable knitted jerseys, others wearing collarless shirts with white or coloured neckerchiefs. The ubiquitous cloth cap was the usual headwear: protective hard hats were still in the future.

MANUFACTURING

The Industrial Revolution brought many new jobs in industry and manufacturing. Before the late nineteenth century workshop and factory workers' clothing mainly comprised regular dress, and special safety gear was not yet a legal requirement, although rudimentary protective workwear evolved in particularly hazardous industries. For centuries metalworkers had used leather aprons as protection from sparks and friction, and these were still worn in the eighteenth century, and, for example, by Victorian iron workers.

Similarly, shipbuilders working with molten metal sometimes used thigh-length leather overtrousers, and hard caps with a deep peak extending over the nose to shield the eyes from the glare. In 1876, at the Great Central Gasworks, retort-house workers used face masks as a barrier against the heat, while for some occupations hard boots with flap fronts protected the feet from molten metal and falling objects. Nonetheless, safety work gear was *ad hoc* and inadequate until the passing of the 1891 Factory and Workshop Act, which enacted various regulations governing dangerous occupations. The Act ruled that chemical works, paint manufacturers, iron-plate enamellers, match and explosives factories, and other industries where workers were exposed to poisonous fumes and injurious substances, should provide 'suitable' respirators, overall suits, and in some cases headwear and gloves.

This boilermaker from Ruston's industrial equipment manufactory in Lincoln, photographed in 1896, wears no special workwear, but a regular lounge suit and bowler hat.

Right: By the early twentieth century some men working in factories and workshops wore protective boiler suits or front-buttoning overall coats, as seen in this 1920s photograph.

Far right: During the First World War 'munitionettes' were initially issued with flame-retardant canvas or cotton-twill belted overall dresses and caps. The triangular badges showed that the wearer was involved in war work.

By the early twentieth century all-in-one trousered overalls of denim or calico were worn by many male factory workers: often called 'mechanics' overalls' or 'boiler suits', these were either made with sleeves or in the dungaree style. Female factory workers also wore overalls, usually a hard-wearing washable cotton long-sleeved overdress to protect the clothes and satisfy basic hygiene requirements, with a cap covering the hair. During the First World War many women took over men's jobs and worked in heavy

Female workers from the Royal Ordnance Factory at Kirkby, near Liverpool, wearing wrap-over overall dresses to protect their everyday clothes, 1944.

industries, from shipbuilding to munitions factories. Initially 'munitionettes' were issued with flame-retardant canvas or cotton-twill front-buttoning overall dresses, but these were soon supplemented with trousers, and from then on women in many wartime occupations wore a shorter, belted overall and trousers. After the war, regulations governing industrial clothing were continually revised and extended: for example, an order of 1921 required those working with acidic solutions to use rubber gloves and aprons of acid-proof material. By the Second World War, when again women assumed many male roles, they wore a range of workwear from overall coats to boiler suits.

TEXTILE WORKERS

As cloth manufacture became increasingly mechanised from the late eighteenth century onwards, many textile workers left their cottage industries to operate machinery in vast mills and factories. The dress of female millworkers broadly followed fashion, but employers could define the boundaries: for example, when girls working in Samuel Courtauld's mills adopted the vast crinoline frame, he declared it to be inconvenient and dangerous when using power looms and winding and drawing engines, and prohibited its wear to work. Consequently dresses worn in textile mills were generally plain, and hemlines usually shorter than fashionable gowns. Initially half-length aprons might be worn, but later a long, sleeveless or short-sleeved bodice of white linen or cotton appeared: reputedly evolving in the mills, this garment, put on over the head, was an early form of pinafore. Hair was often worn in a net, and feet were bare or protected in sturdy wooden-soled clogs.

Male textile workers often worked in their shirt sleeves and trousers, sometimes going barefoot. Some ingenious protective garments were devised for certain processes, such as the apron combined with leg shields, for dyeing and printing cloth. Children also worked in Victorian mills, girls typically wearing shift-like dresses, while boys' clothing followed adult male styles. By the early twentieth century men were beginning to adopt the boiler suits worn in many factories, the safest style when operating machinery, although overall coats were worn in some industries. Mill women's work dresses shortened with the times, rising from ankle to calf and finally knee length by the 1940s; clothing was usually protected by an apron or pinafore.

Some textile processes required specialised workwear. This engraving from *Textile Manufactures of Great Britain* (1844) shows a man dyeing bandanas wearing a protective apron combined with leg shields.

CRAFTS AND TRADES

CARPENTERS

Georgian carpenters wore no special work garments except a half-apron over their clothes, only their tools identifying their trade. Early-nineteenth-century images show carpenters working in their shirt sleeves and breeches, and wearing large aprons, some aprons having pointed bibs buttoned to the shirt front. Heads were bare, or neat skullcaps were worn, but by the Victorian era a paper cap was associated with carpenters, a form of headwear already adopted by such craftsmen and tradesmen as glass-blowers, printers, paper-makers and soap-boilers, encouraged by the lowering cost of paper. Later Victorian photographs depict carpenters and cabinet-makers wearing diverse clothing including regular lounge suits, loose slop-type working jackets, bibbed aprons, and often a cloth tool belt worn around the waist, basic workwear that continued into the early twentieth century.

SMITHS

Smiths had worn protective leather aprons since at least the fourteenth century, and, following tradition, Georgian smiths and farriers generally wore a stout leather apron over their shirts and breeches. The leather apron continued to be worn throughout the nineteenth and early twentieth centuries, protecting the wearer from sparks, functioning as a lap for metal sheets and as a pad for horses' hooves. Sometimes the apron incorporated a square bib secured with shoulder straps, or a pointed bib buttoned to the shirt, the apron skirt often fringed at the bottom or split in the centre, to cover the front of each leg separately. The typical Victorian blacksmith wore a soft cap, but by the early twentieth century many wore the popular working man's cloth cap.

BUTCHERS

An apron was already firmly established as essential for butchers by the eighteenth century. It was either blue, following Butchers' Guild guidelines, or white, and worn over breeches and shirt or sleeved waistcoat. During the

Opposite:
This street vendor from W. H. Pyne's *Costume of Great Britain* (1805) wears layers of coarse clothing, and the blue apron usual for handling animal carcasses.

A rare photograph of the village smithy at Manafon, North Wales, 1894, showing two blacksmiths wearing traditional split leather aprons and soft caps.

Two butcher boys pose for a studio photograph, 1870s. The retouched colour highlights their blue coats and traditional blue and white striped butchers' aprons.

early nineteenth century blue became the more usual apron colour, while blue washable oversleeves protected the coat sleeve from wrist to upper arm. Victorian butchers also tended to wear blue coats or overalls, the colour thereby firmly identifying their trade. By the mid-nineteenth century the blue apron often bore distinctive horizontal white stripes, the width of the stripes theoretically denoting master butcher or apprentice status. The Butchers' Guild also required butchers to wear a hat, and top hats were correct until the 1860s, when many adopted bowler hats. During the 1890s straw boater hats grew popular for summer, and by the century's turn had become so closely associated with butchers that the image of a straw boater often appeared on their trade signs. During the early twentieth century the butcher's frock coat or overall was made of serge, blue jean or bluette, the striped apron usually of jean or cotton drill, and a waterproof oilskin or, later, rubber apron being used for market. After the First World War the white overall coat worn in many food industries became common; it is still worn today by some traditional butchers, with the distinctive blue and white striped apron.

BAKERS AND COOKS

Occupations in which the worker was likely to become covered in flour inspired the wearing of white clothes. For many years bakers and cooks dressed similarly: during the eighteenth and early nineteenth centuries each wore a white linen nightcap and large white apron. Victorian bakers' headwear was very diverse, but eventually the flat tam-o'-shanter-style cap was favoured, the shape being convenient for balancing trays of pastries on the head. From the late eighteenth century male cooks wore a distinctive long-sleeved white waistcoat, effectively a short jacket, its colour initially determined by the natural hue of the linen fabric considered best suited to working in a hot environment. The role of the male chef grew more significant in the nineteenth century, his white clothing, besides being comfortable,

This engraving from the *Book of Trades and Library of Useful Arts* (1811) depicts a baker wearing a linen nightcap and large protective white apron, his shirt sleeves rolled up.

following contemporary recommendations concerning health and hygiene. His outfit was completed by a white apron and cap, which ranged from flat tam-o'-shanter or 'pork pie' shapes to the tall 'cauliflower' style popular in the late nineteenth and early twentieth centuries.

MILKMEN AND MILKMAIDS

The Georgian milkmaid who carried fresh milk into town in pails suspended from a yoke typically wore a bedgown, ankle-length petticoat, large white apron, and a straw bergère hat or felt hat. Some milkmen also operated in town, often wearing the traditional dairyman's rural smock. From 1864 onwards milk was brought into London by train, and, as railways took over the transportation of milk from country to town, a more extensive, organised trade developed. Milk despatched from depots was now delivered to customers' homes by delivery boys or men wearing bibbed blue aprons. By the 1890s Express Dairy milkmen received a company uniform comprising a white buttoned coat with blue lapels and cuffs and a blue apron. Similarly, during the early twentieth century milkmen from large dairies driving a float often wore an overall coat with a plain or blue and white striped apron. However, there remained

A milkmaid illustrated in W. H. Pyne's *Costume of Great Britain* (1805) carries milk into town wearing a coloured petticoat, looped-up bedgown, large white apron, coloured neckerchief, and a straw bergère hat over her cap.

Well-dressed
milkmen wearing
lounge suits, ties,
cloth caps and
aprons prepare
to push handcarts
through the
streets of Hove,
East Sussex,
c. 1910.

During the Second
World War many
women took
on male jobs.
This woman,
photographed
in 1941, wears a
masculine jacket,
shirt and tie with
jodhpurs to deliver
milk from the
local dairy.

considerable variation in dress, some urban milkmen pushing handcarts, dressed in lounge suits teamed with an apron, while rural milkmen driving horse-drawn floats often wore breeches or jodhpurs and boots and gaiters.

STREET VENDORS

Open-air street vendors and traders were a familiar sight until the end of the nineteenth century. Usually aprons were worn over regular garments; blue and green fabric or sacking aprons were usual with vendors selling animal carcasses. Besides protecting clothes, aprons were also useful for carrying wares, the bibs and folded-up apron skirts often being used to hold goods ranging from newspapers to fruit. During the eighteenth century waist belts and sashes were also worn for suspending pouches and receptacles used in the trade, such as the ink-seller's funnel and measuring jug. Hawkers (usually itinerants from the country selling game, poultry, eggs and so on) and vendors of household items such as clothes pegs and brooms, collected from the cottages where they were made, sometimes wore a rural labourer's smock instead of an apron. Working outdoors in all weather, street traders were never without a hat or bonnet.

SHOPWORKERS

Shopworkers generally wore regular dress, and during the eighteenth and nineteenth centuries typically also wore aprons. Protecting the clothes

was a practical necessity for manufacturer-retailers who wore the same apron at the counter as they did at the workbench. Victorian shopkeepers who merely sold goods also customarily wore aprons: for example, ladies visiting smart shoe shops were served by men kneeling before them in aprons. Assistants employed in clothing and drapery shops were expected to look fashionable, yet well-groomed and respectable. During the early twentieth century the apron, with its working-class connotations, was discarded by most shopworkers, except those handling food or working in chemists. Over time the traditional half-length or bibbed white apron was superseded by the washable overall coat, which provided better protection and was more hygienic.

By the twentieth century aprons were usually worn only by shopworkers handling food, like these Edwardian village store staff from Plumpton Green, East Sussex.

These shop assistants working in a Dunfermline, Fife, grocery store during the 1930s wear modern hygienic white overall coats.

61

GLOSSARY

Alpaca: shiny fabric woven with silky wool yarn from the fleece of the alpaca.

Beaver hat: various styles of glossy hat made from felted beaver fur.

Bedgown: cross-over gown of cotton or mixed textiles, worn as a three-quarter-length garment by working women, and usually kept in place by an apron.

Bluette: woollen cloth of bluish colour.

Buckskin: soft animal hide, usually from a buck (male deer), or other specially prepared skins.

Calico: generic term for substantial plain cotton fabrics.

Canvas: heavy-duty unbleached fabric traditionally of linen, later cotton.

Corduroy: warm, durable cotton fabric with ridged or corded surface.

Drabbet: twilled cotton fabric.

Drill: stout cotton fabric.

Flannel: soft woollen fabric with a loose weave.

Frock coat: the main eighteenth- or early-nineteenth-century male garment, featuring a collar.

Fustian: sturdy fabric woven with a linen warp and cotton weft.

Gaiters: heavy cloth or leather leg coverings extending from the instep to the calf or knee.

Jean: hard-wearing twilled cotton fabric often used for working clothes.

Linsey-woolsey: fabric woven with a linen warp and woollen weft.

Moleskin: durable cotton fabric with a soft pile.

Nightcap: informal indoor male cap worn in some occupations.

Pantaloons: very close-fitting calf- or ankle-length trousers.

Petticoat: eighteenth- or early-nineteenth-century term for a skirt.

Plush: type of cotton velvet with a long pile.

Serge: sturdy twilled woollen or worsted cloth.

Shift: basic female linen undergarment.

Zephyr: a lightweight worsted cloth.

FURTHER READING

Ashelford, Jane. *The Art of Dress: Clothes and Society 1550–1914*. National Trust, 1996.

Buck, Anne. *Dress in Eighteenth-Century England*. Harper Collins, 1979.

Cunnington, P., and Lucas, C. *Occupational Costume in England*. A. & C. Black, 1967.

De Marly, Diana. *Working Dress*. Batsford, 1986.

Evans, Siân. *Life Below Stairs in the Victorian and Edwardian Country House*. National Trust, 2011.

Ewing, Elizabeth. *Everyday Dress, 1650–1900*. B. T. Batsford, 1997.

Hannavy, John. *The Victorians and Edwardians at Work*. Shire Publications, 2009.

Lansdell, Avril. *The Clothes of the Cut: A History of Canal Costume*. British Waterways Board, 1975.

Lansdell, Avril. *Occupational Costume*. Shire Publications, 1977.

Levitt, S., and Tozer, J. *Fabric of Society. A Century of People and Their Clothes, 1770–1870*. Laura Ashley, 1983.

Shrimpton, Jayne. *How to Get the Most from Family Pictures*. Society of Genealogists, 2011.

Styles, John. *The Dress of the People*. Yale University Press, 2007.

USEFUL WEBSITES

For such a wide-ranging subject, a great deal of useful information and many relevant images are accessible online. Here are a few recommended websites:

Beamish Living Museum of the North: www.beamish.org.uk

British Postal Museum and Archive: www.postalheritage.org.uk

City of London Police Museum: www.citypolicemuseum.org.uk

Durham Mining Museum: www.dmm.org.uk

Imperial War Museums: www.iwm.org.uk

London Transport Museum: www.ltmuseum.co.uk

Museum of English Rural Life, Reading: www.reading.ac.uk/merl

National Waterways Museum: www.nwm.org.uk

Scottish Fisheries Museum: www.scotfishmuseum.org

INDEX